99A

YOUR SELF INTROSPECTION GUIDE

LUCAS LENIN

ISBN 979-888606213-7

Gratitude

Thank you for Choosing this Book and thanks to the universe for giving me an opportunity to bring it to your hand.

Contents

Contents

Contents

Contents

Preface

This is a classic guide to life success, a better connectivity and self realization. The 99A is all about your self Introspection. This book helps you to settle the life positive way.

CHAPTER ONE

Leadership

Each one of us has the leadership quality hidden within us. It is our inborn quality. Even you have it. It doesn't matter who you are, what work you do or what job you have. You should always be precisely accurate and positive. There will always be a crowd watching you. But, ignoring those watchful eyes, you should be mindful about yourselves. You should not forget that in case you happen to do a mistake, even your subordinate will notice you. Take the reins of your life in your own hands, rise above the situations you face, make a plan for yourself and make sure you follow it. If you feel necessary, without hesitation, seek advice from a qualified person.

CHAPTER TWO

Service

Leadership itself can be a service. Without any hesitation, you should share your knowledge openly with your co-workers and your subordinates. You should not have the slightest doubt or insecurity, that if you share your knowledge, they may rise above you. If you bear such an open mindset, you yourself will have the opportunity to learn a lot of new things. This attitude will help you identify the true nature of people clearly. This further will create a path for a lot of people to approach you and be your true friends. You can only reap what you sow. So try to do service without expecting benefits in return.

CHAPTER THREE

Habit of Reading Books

You should never take it that your learning process has ended with schools and colleges. In fact, you start learning a lot soon after college. It is not possible for you to attempt the college examination by studying just +2. In the same way, you cannot attempt the exam of life just by finishing the college syllabus. If you happen to inculcate the habit of reading books, on any topic, be it exercise, cooking, sports, financial management, short stories, self-development or spiritual, whatever be it, you should make it a habit to read daily. Make it a point to read at least one page. Reading enthusiastically whatever you like will give you immense pleasure. That joy cannot be controlled by others. It's all solely yours. As you make reading a habit, you will be able to reign over your emotions. Gradually, this ability becomes ingrained in you.

Later, even when the authors of the books fade away in time, their timeless thoughts, opinions and philosophy will prevail over you.

CHAPTER FOUR

Create a Difference

It's generally wise not to hold a judgemental attitude in any situation. You should hold a stance to encourage whatever right has to be done. Finding faults with family or friends is easy. But in such situations, you should be the one to affectionately and patiently guide your people to the desired righteous path. Now, this is an arduous task. So, most people refrain from doing this. However, you should have the capability to develop yourself to be able to create a difference. Be distinguished.

CHAPTER FIVE

Keep a Smiling Face

Our smile tends to fade away with age. However, you should try and smile more often as you age. As you grow older, you will have more and more responsibilities and pressures. Succumbing to those, you would be unable to control your emotions in a graceful manner. Then, after sometime, you often tend to regret our behaviour and words.

Well, when you want to discuss with some people and make a decision, would you prefer to do it with a calm, gentle and smiling person, who is approachable or a person with a red face? You would obviously approach a gentle and smiling person. So is the case with everyone else. You should be the change you want to see in others. You should change yourself to become the same way you expect others to be. Keep smiling.

CHAPTER SIX

Stand Strong and Brave

Never except your life to be a smooth path for you. Everyone on this planet has just 24hours, just like you do. So, you should stress yourself being reminiscent of your past or you shouldn't ponder over the future either. You should remember that if something is meant to be yours, it will be yours ultimately. However, it is also true that, if you do not put in any effort to achieve it, then it won't wait for you either. So, stand strong and brave in believing that you can achieve it.

CHAPTER SEVEN

Help Others and Be Happy

On a day to day basis, you do think, "What dress do I wear today?" At least for 5secs per day. At a restaurant, you play with the menu card, being indecisive about what you want to order, you would take at least 10secs to order. Then, planning about where to go for a weekend trip definitely takes some hours.

However, you should remember that there are people around us who do not have options like this. You should extend whatever help you can to such people. You should care for such helpless people around you as much as you can. Over a period of time, your tendency to help and care for those around you will increase and their thankfulness will transform and enrich your life abundantly. Help others for your own happiness.

CHAPTER EIGHT

Act Together

The situation we are in today, knowingly or unknowingly, we tend to become a Position-conscious individual. We often tend to look down on certain jobs, considering them below our position. Some people even unknowingly leave their current position in their quest for the next higher position. But they do not realise that if they do well and give results in their current position, the next higher position, for which they aware aspiring for so badly, will automatically come to them. Whatever position you are in, you need to work together with your co-workers . Acting together will help all the individuals in the team to alleviate their positions together.

CHAPTER NINE

Organize Yourself

If you are told to descend a ten storey building via steps, you can easily descend. However, if you were asked to climb, it would be a hard task for you. In the same way, learning a good habit takes time and effort. However, bad habits are generally easy and stick on soon. Whatever activity you do, you should be consistent in it. Only then it will be a regular habit. Self discipline is the first step to success.

CHAPTER TEN

Plan Your Day

Organise your life as well as you can. Make it a habit to write down your work plan and to-do chores list every day morning. Try to complete your list on the same day. If you procrastinate, your list for the next day will be longer than usual. The previous day's chores will get accumulated. You can keep a weekly planner or even a monthly planner. But, be mindful that if an activity or a chore which could have been completed in a day, is extended over a week or month, planning itself will not be effective.

CHAPTER ELEVEN

Be Honest

Just because someone is keeping a watch over you in our society, you should not develop an inferiority complex or a superiority complex. If you do, you are pressuring yourself. You should live a satisfactory life for yourself. People, who think small, try to copy others and work towards becoming like them. Instead, you should be truthful and honest to people around you. Imitating someone else never does any good. You should try to overcome your shortcomings as soon as possible. You should work towards improving your shortcomings at least one per day, everyday. Being honest to self leaves room to realise and improve self.

CHAPTER TWELVE

Take care of Your Health

You can say that your body is a live machine. Many machines in your home would have gone through repair and maintenance phases. However, you must have observed that post repair, their efficiency and performance decrease considerably. You have to take care of your own body. During ill health, your family can take care of you, but for a limited period of time. After that, it becomes a burden to them. It's not that your family, relatives or friends can lend you a part of their body for some time and take it back later. Isn't it? That's the main reason why you should take care of your health. Health should be your priority always.

CHAPTER THIRTEEN

Despair

Do you share a bitter relationship with anyone? Do you bear vengeance towards someone because they have been badmouthing you or scolding you? Have you vowed to see the end of the person? Well, this is equal to you tying down a 5kg rock to your leg and trying to walk by dragging it along. And, additionally if you try to take along others worries and strained feelings, then you are dragging along another rock too. Your mind might often say, "how can you forget it so easily, when it has caused so much of pain to you?" However, your intellect will be ever ready to forgive. Just give it a thought, all this time, when you have burdened yourself with all the despair and vengeance, what did you gain? So, for things that do not matter much, why bear the burden? If you release yourself off your burdens, you will be able to walk ahead towards your aim with a clear head.

CHAPTER FOURTEEN

Conflict – A Part of Life

Encountering a conflict in any situation or discussion in inevitable. In some situations, giving up the conflict and moving on would be wise. And sometimes, not knowing what to do and escaping the situation may seem like a better option for that moment, but that may not be a good decision on a long run. Many a time, even a small argument about who might be correct, may turn into a huge conflict. You should bear in mind that conflicts, small or large are all an inevitable part of life. That certainly doesn't mean that you should argue your heart out and win the verbal battle. You should either have a big heart, enough to say, “you are right” and make the other person happy or you must improvise your exceptional convincing abilities and make the other person see through your point.

CHAPTER FIFTEEN

Take care of Relationships

Friends are often the first people in our lives to walk us along paths of life... be it right or wrong. Our forefathers have said that if you are in a good companionship, you would tread along a good path in your life. People, who meet us in our day-to-day life, influence us in various ways, even without our knowledge. Their small actions attract us considerably and it becomes ingrained into our memory so much so that we tend to act the same way. So you must consciously classify the people around you into positive attitude ones and negative attitude ones. Try to stay away from people with negative attitude a little bit. You'll feel enthusiastic and inspirational by surrounding yourself with people with positive attitude and good vibes. So, now u knows which way to go. Make sure to build healthy relationships around yourself.

CHAPTER SIXTEEN

Motivation or Activation

Have u ever noticed yourself being influenced by intoxicating people? You were being motivated by them. For e.g. you look at some of your friends or relatives or colleagues and notice that he/ she have a smart dressing sense or someone riding a stylish bike. You saw someone a while ago, wearing sunglasses. You think it was awesome! You get inspired by others and you try to replicate the same ways or things in your life. Your friends or your close associates are often the exact people whom, you unconsciously follow or try to become into. So, unknowingly you tread into the same path, be it right or wrong. That's why it is important to be in good companionship and to be able to classify the real nature of the people around you. You can get influenced or motivated by the people you surround yourself with.

CHAPTER SEVENTEEN

Use Pause Button

Do you consider yourself a busy person who has a lot on his/her plate and has to keep hurrying around? Do you always complain of running short of time and hence not being able to complete the work? In that case, you should realise one thing. If you push yourself to work without a rest, then, over a period of time, your brain and body will get used to the mindful stress. The only futile remainder is your entire body becoming tired. But, it doesn't stop there. Just because you became tired or sick, the work to be done or the company will not stop. There will surely be someone else to complete it. There will be someone who will replace you. On the other hand, if you work on time on relax by taking a small break; you will be able to work more efficiently with better results. Now, isn't that what you want? So, take a break at times and relax at regular intervals. Take care of your health, physically and mentally.

CHAPTER EIGHTEEN

Are you Ready to Invest in This way

Every one of us learns things at various phases of our lives. Have you ever shared your knowledge with others without expecting anything in return? Please think once this way. For e.g. when you are sharing a fact or concept with me, I happen to notice some obscure detail in it and I mention it to you. Then we discuss it further. That is, you get to understand the concept in a more detailed manner. This shows that whenever you invest your time for sharing your knowledge, you help others and simultaneously help yourself to grow quickly.

CHAPTER NINETEEN

Are you growing?

What's with this question? Are you thinking so? Well, this question is not regarding your physical age. Not even about your teenage, marriage or family life. After your studies at school and college, what new have you done to learn or gain knowledge? Do you have any dream, ambition or goal? If yes, how much effort have you put in pursuing the goal? If you have worked continually and consistently, is the result of your work noticed to be better and improved? If u find yourself moving a step closer to your goal or the result of your work is noticeably good and being applauded within your company at least, and if all of this gives you a sense of joy and fulfilment, only then, it means that you are growing towards success. Now let's consider answering the question again. Do u think you are growing up in the right direction?

CHAPTER TWENTY

Visualise

"I had a mango yesterday, but it was quite souring. But the tamarind was exquisiteness tasty. It had a kind of sweet-sour taste, which left me craving for more." Often, people start drooling just by hearing or even reading this kind of lines. Some people even imagine themselves eating the same. This is the kind of dream that stimulates your emotions to achieve your goal. Let's just run a few minutes of visualisation process with emotions of our dream achieved and the daily routine we put in to achieve it. Visualise it every day. That itself will motivate you to run towards your ambition.

CHAPTER TWENTY-ONE

Work out for Your Goal

We all would have had some of the other ambition. There will be a goal for everyone to achieve in their lifetime. Some people often tend to procrastinate by thinking that a better time or a right time will come or a right day will come to travel towards it or start it. Well, I say let's start now. However big your dream may be, break it into smaller achievable targets, place a deadline for every step and put a sincere effort for it. It's not necessary that our effort or attempt is perfect. The fact that you have tried itself is all that counts. The result will become as expected and perfect automatically with your consistent efforts.

CHAPTER TWENTY-TWO

Have Commitment

Visualising your dream, creating small achievable targets and going for it is all acceptable. But, if you lack the commitment, you will not be consistent. And will not be able to reach your goal. Isn't it? For e.g. you dream of living in a debt- free lavish lifestyle. You also have a personal loan. Let's say, in the middle of the EMI schedule you get an offer for a top-up on your loan. If you avail the top-up, then it means that you have no commitment towards paying off your loan and your dream. You dream of being debt-free and rich but on the other hand, you are increasing your loan amount. It doesn't sound right. Does it? There will be many a distractions while working out for your dream project (like that of the top up loan). But, your mind should not oscillate and you should be strong on your purpose.

CHAPTER TWENTY-THREE

How to Self-Estimate Properly?

Well, let me tell you a small incident from my office which happened the other day. I gave my team a small test- judge yourself and give you marks out of 100.

60 people took the test. Out of them all, only one person gave himself 100/100. Instantly, all the others started to laugh sarcastically at him. To this, he replied, "If I undervalue myself, won't it be like me underestimating myself?" Well, that's exactly right. We all have our own strengths and weaknesses. If we focus on our strengths alone, it's enough to overcome the weaknesses.

CHAPTER TWENTY-FOUR

Being Afraid to Face Failure

A lot of us would have tried and would have put continued efforts many times. And must have failed many times too. The failures may have resulted in financial losses, loss of relations, time or work. Thus, there starts a cold fear in our minds about facing losses. The fear we accumulate from the losses prevents us from taking the next step to success. When we think of starting a fresh, the pain of the losses in the past starts pulling us back, creating fear about facing loss again. However, the first thing we need to eliminate is, fear.

CHAPTER TWENTY-FIVE

Sacrifice for Others

Have you ever noticed? There are a set of people around you in the society... Do you know their beauty? They can procure the things they want from you very easily. You end up pitying them easily and be ready to do whatever it takes to help them out. You may see it as a sacrifice or a help you are doing to them. But, the real time picture is that, they are exploiting you. Leeching you off.

CHAPTER TWENTY-SIX

Do Not Lament

Lamenting has become a common habit for most people nowadays. People tend to lament tirelessly about an event of the past. Even if someone tries to persuade them away from the topic saying, "it's alright. It's a thing of past now.", they often reply, "you should be in my place to know my pain." However, one thing is true. By lamenting, you cannot rewrite the history in your favour. But, lamenting sure does destroy the upcoming possible result of a future event. If your actions and words are pessimistic, only negative or undesired things happen. So, staying optimistic does help you in the long run.

CHAPTER TWENTY-SEVEN

Love Yourself

If you notice people who work well, you would understand. Some of them put aside their dreams and do what it takes, to fulfil the needs of his relations and family. He would consider doing it all for his self-satisfaction. But, he too would have needs, dreams, and ambitions. He/she should not stagnate his/her own aspirations. He/she should strive for it along with other duties and responsibilities, should take steps to make them happen. To put it in a simple way- you can only share love if you love yourself.

CHAPTER TWENTY-EIGHT

Success Journey

We have seen people who have failed in their first attempt. We have even seen people who have failed after multiple continuous attempts. But, in my opinion, those people have not failed. Their success has just been postponed for a while. That's all. People who are talented and skilled tend to dally with the excuse of lack of time. People who are talented, knowledgeable and have time, tend to dawdle around with the excuse of lack of money. People, who have it all, just say that they do not have the mindset to do the activity.

Such people, who dodge things, keep themselves comfortable and search of lame excuses. When you give up those lame excuses, stop procrastinating and start the activity, your journey to success begins at that very moment.

CHAPTER TWENTY-NINE

Renew the Contacts

Check the number of people you have on your contacts list on your mobile phone. Is it 500+ or 1000+ or even more? Out of all those list of contacts, , how many people are you actually in touch with? How many people are you regularly contacting for business, relations or family? May be you will be able to count the number on your fingers. Then what about the rest of the contacts? You have kept them just in case, they may be necessary in the future. Well, that day however, never does arrive. Even if such a day comes, they may not give you the same importance or value which you would have expected. It becomes obvious to you that with passing time, lot have changed. So, if you practice calling and talking to at least one person weekly/ monthly you will be able to develop a good relationship. The power of staying in touch and keeping in contact will definitely show up in the future.

CHAPTER THIRTY

Measure Yourself

People often complain of not having enough time. Sometimes you feel it yourselves. So, let's do a small exercise for it. Have a paper and a pen with you around for about a week. Note down the starting time and ending time of each activity you do every day. Review at the end of the week. Tick the work which you feel is productive. And cross the unproductive part. You will realise on the 7th day that how much unproductive work you have been doing.

CHAPTER THIRTY-ONE

Are You Talented?

People keep learning new things. We see our friends and relatives taking up new hobbies and learning things. But on asking a doubt or a fact or something, they deny knowing the answer. Instantly, we misunderstand that they are knowingly refusing to tell. Well, there is a saying by an American writer Gladwell that for a person to be an expert in a particular field, he/ she needs to work on that particular concept or subject or job for at least 10000 hours. Now let me ask you, do you still think that the person who refused to answer you previously, was an expert? May be he really wasn't sure of an answer to your question.

If you have been working on a particular field for many years and have gained sufficient knowledge and experience regarding the same, then try to create a service. Try to impart that knowledge to many people in an open minded manner. This service you do will automatically push you in a favourable direction.

CHAPTER THIRTY-TWO

What do you need to focus on?

Everyone in this world has a problem of some kind..they all have to face some unfavourable situation at some point of their time. Majority of the people focus only on the problem , pondering more and more over it. Instead, they should have searched for the root cause of the problem and focused on finding a solution to it. You achieve whatever you concentrate and focus on. For eg. If you are driving a car or bike, you see a pothole on the left side of the road. Instantly, you would turn right and prefer to drive on a smooth road. But, if you keep driving over the pothole, you wouldn't be able to take the better road.

So, is there a justification for your thinking and actions and another for the problems in your life? It can't be so. Isn't it?

If you are dealing with a problem or conflict in life, please focus on finding a solution to it rather than pondering over it.

CHAPTER THIRTY-THREE

What is the Right Kind of Help?

Sometimes, we think about how can we be of some help to our loved ones..how can we benefit them in some way or the other. Or how can we extend some favour to some NGO or someone else. Sometimes, we take a step ahead and reach out to extend some assistance to them. Hearty congratulations to those people.

If you ever faced a problem or difficulty in life, you would have had an action plan to solve it and had a problem free life. Similarly, you have a lot of people around you with similar situations and helplessness. If you share your methods and strategies to overcoming at least some of their worries, they too would be relieved to some extent. They would be extremely thankful to you.

In my opinion, this is an example of a proper help or assistance you could extend to your loved ones.

CHAPTER THIRTY-FOUR

What Kind of Person are you?

We all have two types of solutions to face any situation in life. First is, putting in continuous effort, being brave and strong, keep trying till your desired result is achieved. Secondly, keep trying, but if you do not see any favourable results, then quit. Which one of these types are you?

If you belong to the first type, you will definitely achieve all your goals and fulfil your ambitions. If you belong to the second, you will live with whatever life has to offer you.

So, now you can decide which type you belong to.

CHAPTER THIRTY-FIVE

Do not Allow Thoughts to be Imposed

Let's recollect the events in our lives. Everyone of us would have thought about our life ambition for at least a few times. But would not have decided on it. For eg. When you were in school, your teacher must have asked us all ," hey students! Let's talk about ambitions. Tell me one by one about your ambition in life." Next, before you take your 10th class examination, your teachers and parents advice you that this exam is very important and is the base for your life. The marks obtained in this exam will facilitate your entry into any suitable group of your choice in +1. So, at that point of time, your ambition will be to score good marks in your 10th class exam. Next, during your +2exams, the same thing repeats. And this time it's about professional college and career. Beyond all this, there would be something that you decided upon while in college. But in the end, when you get to work in the reality of life, you realise that there is absolutely no relation between what you were thinking about and what the reality is.

This is one life you get to have. Do not allow others to impose their views on you. For that, you should have the maturity to take your own decisions. Taking advice from people is good. But letting others impose their decisions on you shouldn't be acceptable.

CHAPTER THIRTY-SIX

What is Ambition?

I remember, I had organised a team meet at my office. There were a total of 10 people. I asked them what their ambition was? Some of them wanted to buy a house, some wanted to pay off their debts, some wanted to buy a car and gift it to their parents, take them around for a ride in it, etc. But one person said that he wanted to start a business. So, I replied to them all that whatever they all said about buying house, car, paying off debts, is all their responsibility. So what about their ambition?

Your ambition should be something which keeps you driving ahead, makes you better each day, creates a thirst for knowledge in you and makes to implement that knowledge for your own betterment.

CHAPTER THIRTY-SEVEN

Goals

I remember, I met an old friend of mine and we started talking for a long time. From all that discussion, I learnt one thing. He has reached his goal at a cost. He had to sacrifice lots of things, had to overcome office politics and a lot more to become the General Manager of the company. I heartily congratulated him on his achievement, talent and growth. Then, I asked him,"what next?" I asked him what his next ambition would be. But then, there was absolute silence from his end. He did not have any next goals.

In my opinion, you need not have just one goal. There is no such law. Being able to achieve a goal is appreciated. Then, you can have your next goal. Life is a journey. People who have the satisfaction of fulfilment of at least one of their ambitions are lucky.

CHAPTER THIRTY-EIGHT

Expressing Comments

This may happen with you or with someone near you. You must have noticed that most of the time, you tend to show a laid- back attitude when it comes to dealing with yourself. Sometimes, you have an idea about a concept, but being unsure of how good it is or how perfect it is, u do not share it and keep it to yourselves. Gradually, this feeling decreases.

But then, how do you feel when after some days, someone else gets appreciated for similar idea? In fact, you feel that your thought process and idea was better than his. Then you might feel that you should have shared your idea previously instead of hiding it. Then you would be appreciated instead of the other person.

Now this is a good thought. You should go beyond that hesitation and be open to sharing your knowledge and ideas. No one knows which idea of yours might turn out to be a huge break for you.

So, are you ready to share your thoughts and ideas at your work place without hesitation?

CHAPTER THIRTY-NINE

Thought Box

Sometimes, you come up with an idea that the result of the project report which you worked on previously, might have been better if some small changes were made. Some businessmen think that if they had fine-tuned some processes, their project outcomes would have been more fruitful. But then, as soon as you enter your office or workplace or sit at your desk, the idea seems to evaporate. Your mind goes blank. This can be quite troublesome. So, to avoid such situations, I suggest you should note it down somewhere as soon as you get an idea. So u might want to carry a small pocket diary or voice recorder or a mobile phone with you. At the same time, while writing, if you elaborate the idea a little bit , it might be easier when implementing it.

CHAPTER FORTY

Expressing Love

Our mind and intellect do not always express the same thoughts. The mind works well with feelings like love and affection. However, our intellect always weighs the right and wrong / good and bad in any situation. For eg. When you go shopping, your loving life partner, your friends or your adorable parents might come to your mind. You would instantly feel like running around wildly in search of some of their favourite things to gift them. But then, your intellect starts chirping in your brain saying that the cash in your purse might not be sufficient for all the gifts you want to buy at that instant.

Following intellect and wisdom often leads us to think twice in any situation. Gifting expensive items are not always a way to express your love.

CHAPTER FORTY-ONE

Is the Comparison Good?

We all have this habit of comparing. Comparing ourselves with others in various fields. Then when we find something better than ourselves, we tend to feel envious. However, you should find your area of interest and develop yourself in that field. If u compare yourself with others and dream to implement their idea to prosper just like them, then you must be ready to work like them as well. By comparing yourself and feeling envious, you would only spoil your life. On the other hand, based on your talent, skill and interest, strive to develop yourself. Your life is in your hands. You can make it as beautiful as you want.

CHAPTER FORTY-TWO

Conquer your self

Since your childhood, you must have been compared with your friend in class.. saying that he got a certain amount of marks and you too should score the same or more in the next test. When you grow up and start working, you might be compared to your colleague who was once your classmate, by saying that he is positioned in a better job and gets better salary compared to you. So you should match up to him by earning similar or perhaps more. In my opinion , comparing yourself like that does you no good. Rather than a mindset to compete with others like this, our goal should be to raise our targets. Practice to win yourself over and hope for your success.

CHAPTER FORTY-THREE

What is Success?

Each of us has a unique definition of what success is. There are numerous books and articles about the topic SUCCESS, but many people aren't clear about it yet. When you try to study a particular topic, you should study it till you get a clear understanding of the subject. You must keep simulating your success. For eg. You want to become a teacher in a particular subject. So, your next step will be to pursue a course related to the field. For that, you will search a college to study in and to achieve that desire. Since you studied it out of your own interest, you are bound to excel in your studies and reach a good position.

So, it does take quite a lot of planning and preparation to succeed in a particular field or job. Similarly, to go headlong into the field of life and emerge as a winner, you would need quite a lot of basic planning.

Whoever plans his daily chores and achieves his goals, his every achievement becomes a success.

CHAPTER FORTY-FOUR

Who are really Your Friends?

Your motto should be : Tell me who your friend is and I'll tell you who you are. Be it at work place or somewhere outside, you do spend a lot of time with your friends. Discussions and shared thoughts and ideas with your friends might work as a stepping stone for your growth. So, do you find the time spent with your friends worthwhile? Well, there is nothing wrong in chatting with your friends and having a fun filled time with them together. But, while working, if you notice some of your colleagues, you would find them to be very toxic. Their ideas, attitude or even the way they see you do not go down very well with you. So, the best you do is to avoid such people gracefully.

However, even if you are not paying attention, stay away from those people.

CHAPTER FORTY-FIVE

How is Your Mind?

When you want to do a new work or start something afresh, you would have decided it and then started it. If you start to do something, do it wholeheartedly, with a complete mind. Some people however do work for name sake without any interest or happiness. If you do something in half mind, without interest, how will u expect it to turn out well and good. If u do something with interest and believing that you can, its result will be exceptionally good.

CHAPTER FORTY-SIX

Do you know that you are Intelligent?

Your thoughts often change into your actions. Your actions determine your end result, be it good or bad. If the results are good, we are all happy. If otherwise, you become extremely depressed. Our life is a chain of thoughts and actions. Intelligent people surround themselves with good company and tend to impart happiness to people around. In whatever difficult situation they face, the next second they change themselves happy. They do not ponder over their losses. Now, what about you?

CHAPTER FORTY-SEVEN

Your Vision

In a company, when a new manager joined, on the second day of his joining, after introducing all the HOD's, in the hall of the company, while going on a walk with one manager, he said,“ there comes one person. He won't do anything or any work. Just comes and goes. He won't do anything even upon saying. He must have come to watch us.” Saying this he went away. I replied- ok. After sometime, when I came across him again, I asked him,“ sir, would you please tell me where the water dispenser is.” He replied, “ down the hall." Then I complimented him saying that his dressing style is very decent and stylish. He smiled and thanked me for the same and left. Then, the other manager came up to me and asked how he was responding well only to you. To that I replied, "you had seen him as a bad person. But I was optimistic about him. So he would respond to me quite well from now. Even though you were badmouthing about him, I didn't keep it in mind and appreciated him. "

So, what about you? Do you see the good in people or are you otherwise?

CHAPTER FORTY-EIGHT

Do you Value this?

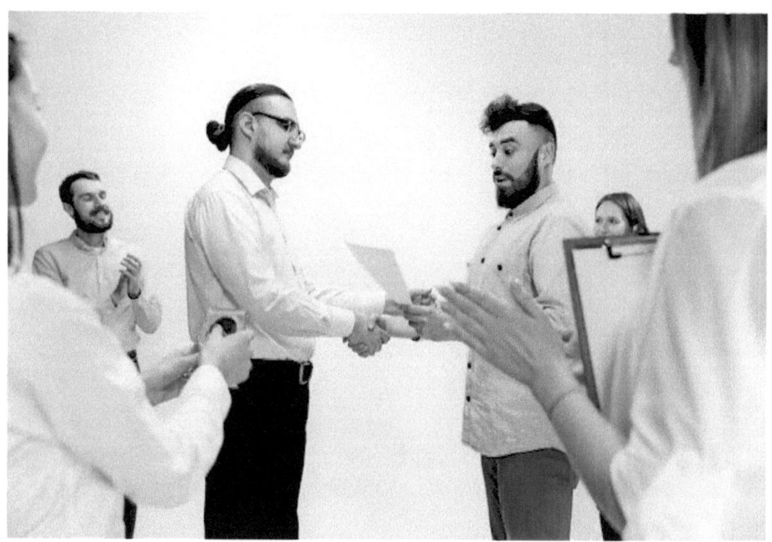

About 10 yrs ago my manager arranged a department meeting. At that meeting, we talked about many of the department's problems and determined the solutions. The meeting ended with me addressing a problem that had not been solved for many years. I asked if anyone had a solution to it, they may meet me the following day and let me know.

The following month, at the factory's inaugural meeting, our manager was awarded with a shield and certificate for resolving a long lasting multiyear problem.

One of my close associate, who was beside me, informed me that the solution to the problem was actually given by another employee. But, instead of him, this manager is getting recognition.

If you appreciate the talent and innovative thinking of people, you too will learn something valuable.

CHAPTER FORTY-NINE

How much More?

How many years have you worked for until today? 5 or 10 or may be more. Have you planned any investments for the future? Have you planned your retirement or have you saved up enough for later?

My friend's father expired recently. He was in quite a good position, earned $1500+ as a monthly income. He lived quite a lavish lifestyle. However, he didn't seem to invest in anything though. Neither did he have any savings.

My friend however got shocking news that he had a number of bad loans to his name. So much so, that he had to go bankrupt.

It doesn't matter whether you are borrowing for your future or to secure your children's future. You should leave your next generation with happiness and assets. Not with loans and burdens. So, learning to handle money smarter might do good to yourself and your future generations.

CHAPTER FIFTY

Fear of Hesitation?

You would have noticed a few people at your workplace. They are really reluctant to make any decisions. They avoid making any decisions till the last minute. At times, even you would have some problems with something and would seek approval of your seniors. In such a case, if they do not give you a proper answer, saying neither ok nor not ok, you ought to feel listlessly impatient.

So, just give this a thought.. have you ever help any of your subordinates in your team without hesitation, at any point of time? Hesitation does not allow you to take a decision. So, try giving up being hesitant and emerge victorious.

CHAPTER FIFTY-ONE

How do you implement a Decision?

Many of us love to make New Year resolutions and would flaunt them on that single day. While some people do not even know about the existence of a concept called New Year Resolutions. The most popular resolutions are : I'll exercise daily and maintain a healthy body, I'll quit drinking etc. However determined might they sound, if you look at them after a few weeks into the New Year, they would have already called quits.

According to a study by University of Scranton, only 8 out of 100 people adhere to their resolutions. The other 92 fail. You do not need to wait for a New Year's Eve or an occasion to make a fresh good start or to give up a bad habit. Let's start now. Let's make it today. It doesn't matter how many resolutions you have listed. Even if it's just one, adhering to the resolution is what that matters.

CHAPTER FIFTY-TWO

Who did not?

Most of us feel guilty about the fact that we know a certain thing very well but still we cannot do it. This guilty conscience follows us through. However, you should understand that everyone does make mistakes. No one seems to be perfect. Once you understand this, taking your next step seems fairly easy. Sometimes, you naturally tend to be a bit lazy. This might give us some temporary failures. But, you should take note that you are just one of all the people who do mistakes from time to time, naturally. It's usually wise to quit feeling guilty for our failures and step ahead with positivity.

CHAPTER FIFTY-THREE

Is this a Garbage Bin?

I remember, my boss and I were preparing a proposal for a project. We worked in the office till 11p.m, got the report prepared and left for our homes. The next morning at 11a.m, when I was in the office, my colleague came and informed me that my boss was asked me to appear in the meeting room urgently. So I hurried to the room. There I found the managers of all departments gathered and my manager was busily searching for the work file which we had completed the previous night. Our General Manager asked me,“did you people work on the report yesterday?” I replied, “ yes sir. We completed it. ”Then he asked why was my manager searching so much for it. Getting frustrated, our GM dismissed the meeting and left. I asked my manager to give me one minute to search for the file. But, I successfully handed it to him in 30secs. At this, my manager was extremely happy.

Be it our work station or computer or house, instead of throwing around things like a garbage bin, being organised save you time, effort and of course respect!

CHAPTER FIFTY-FOUR

Going Forward

A big enterprise today must have begun as a small humble business. Big companies often started out with small workforce. But some people, being unable to make that small beginning, throw excuses of lack of opportunities, time or money.

Starting out small, achieving victory, and from the experience gained, trying to make it out in a big way is usually a wise way to go. Sometimes, we come across people who want to start big, otherwise would not want to start at all. In such cases, the idea never goes forward. You should believe that your small action today might spark up your future. If you are giving up or killing it in the beginning, that means you are directly killing your future dream too. If today's small thoughts are nurtured, it may be the foundation for tomorrow's successful empires.

CHAPTER FIFTY-FIVE

Do This

Recently I read an article survey stating a shocking truth that on an average, we spend 2.5 hrs per day unproductively on social media. So I decided to check it and I consciously started monitoring myself. Surprisingly I found the report to be absolutely true.

So, I decided that I really needed to learn to do things the right way. Make a time frame fix for your daily routine. Chart out your unproductive time.

Once you learn to distinguish between the productive and the unproductive hours, you will be able to master time management.

CHAPTER FIFTY-SIX

Give Importance to Yourself

Most people give priority to money. Recently, a friend of mine had been to an interview. He was asked, "how do you organise your personal life?" So he answered describing his daily routine. The officer replied, "Everything you said is true. But I do not know if you care about your physical health. If you were so focused, your body weight should have been in proportion to your height.

". My friend was obviously overweight. Then he was asked about the dress he was wearing, that how many years ago did he buy it. My friend answered 3years ago. At last the officer dismissed him citing that in their company, they firmly believe that anyone who values his/ her health and appearance will contribute to the growth of their organisation.

If you are not able to take care of yourself, how can you take care of the company you are working at?

CHAPTER FIFTY-SEVEN

Which Job is best?

The strength of one's talent is determined by his ability to deal with the problem he is facing. Very few people actually choose a challenging job. When given a choice, chances are there that 9 out of 10 people will choose an easy job. During interviews, candidates do say that they are looking out for an exciting and challenging career, but in reality, when offered one, only 1% of them would actually be willing to take it up.

There may be various reasons for it. Challenging jobs often demand extra time and effort. The hard work you have to put in tests the level of patience you have.

You will surely face problems when you choose a challenging job. Experiencing the problems will offer you opportunities to find new solutions. This further heightens the strength of your ability.

CHAPTER FIFTY-EIGHT

Accept as It is

I have seen some people pondering and envying others thinking, "if only I had a life like his". He/ she don't even know whether the person he is envying is really enjoying his life or not. Each of us is as unique as our fingerprint. It doesn't matter how unique you are created, you need to work hard to develop the ability which you are good at. You have been created with an efficient physical body. You may be wondering if the current situation you are in is for a purpose. It may not be what it seems to be at all.

If you accept yourself the way you were created, your will develop indomitable confidence in yourself. That itself will lay the path for your next step.

CHAPTER FIFTY-NINE

Prior Advertising?

One of my friends has a strict policy for himself. If someone seeks his help, he would not refuse it. He would try his best to help the person out. But then, he also had the habit of showing off. He would relate the incident to his acquaintances. For eg. Whenever time permits, he would refer to our colleague saying that he couldn't do a job and had asked for help. In that case it was he who did the job for him.

One day when he was talking about a friend like this, I interrupted. In my opinion, people who are experiencing loneliness should try to recover. Instead if they wallow in their own sadness, they would experience more failure.

If you helped someone, that itself is sufficient to have a strong relationship with the person. He / she would be ever thankful to you. You do not need to advertise to everyone about your nature or about the person who received your favours.

CHAPTER SIXTY

Try Creating

Isn't excessive desire for things the root cause of one's destruction? You might aspire for a good job and a decent salary. Business men aspire for a smooth and debt free profit making business. People who earn doing small jobs too aspire similarly. But, if you do not work continuously and sincerely for it, that will not work out. A strong desire to obtain everything in a short period of time will result in loss of your existing job. That might even act as the final nail in the coffin. For eg. The well known social media platform like Facebook is currently available in morethan 110 languages worldwide. It was launched by Mark Zuckerberg in 2004. If he was greedy to launch it in different languages at the same time, would we have its global development and presence today?

Can you create a product or something that others can use.? Try hard to create something useful and meaningful to others.

CHAPTER SIXTY-ONE

The Reason for Everything

I have a friend whose father runs a money lending business in his hometown. He used to pay really low interest rates even if someone asked for help. His strategy was different. He would never demand monthly interest. He would wait until the deadline as stated by the document with the borrower, and then he would register the property which was mortgagedto his name.

He was a real disgrace to the people around him. The reason for his behaviour may be greed, not being able to handle money or even his own financial difficulties. The greed for money makes people do inhumane things.

CHAPTER SIXTY-TWO

You can achieve anything

A wise person once said that if you can rein your emotions, you can achieve anything you want. For eg. You had a wild argument with your boss. At that point of time, you might want to leave the job altogether. But, imagine the situation otherwise. If you had an argument with your subordinate. You would feel angry that he didn't even deem his position and dared to argue with you, who is his higher official. You feel like sacking him to teach him a lesson.

In such situations, instead of feeding your ego, you should handle your emotions maturely. Only then you can change the situation. According to a research report, 57% of divorces result due to conflict of interest. If you can handle your emotions and feelings properly, you can achieve anything.

CHAPTER SIXTY-THREE

Power of the Mind

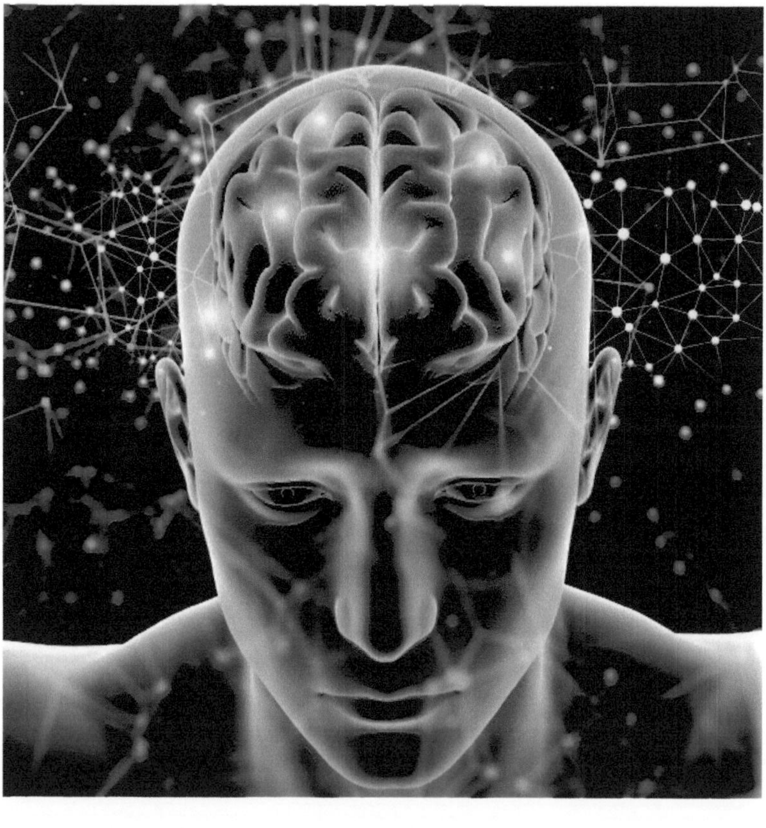

Has anyone told you not to deceive yourself? You might be wondering what does this even mean. This means that sometimes you tend to procrastinate even the smallest things by saying that you cannot do it. Every action of yours has 2 phases. One is when is getting conceived in your thoughts and second is when you actually implement your thoughts.

Being true to yourself, you should often conduct a self analysis on yourself. You should be comparing yourself to all the great men in the society who have admirable achievements to their name. That is because of the power of their mind. The human mind has indomitable strength. It will help you achieve everything you want if you steer it in the right direction.

CHAPTER SIXTY-FOUR

Don't You Know?

I Remember, I attended my friend's wedding which was taking place in a temple. A friend of mine who had accompanied me said that we should just pray in the temple and leave. While praying, I observed that he had been praying for an extraordinarily long time. I smiled and asked, "what is the long list you have been praying now?". To that, he answered, "I have an upcoming transfer in my office. I do not want it. My younger sister and her husband are having some problems. I do not want them to get separated. ". He kept on going with some other things like this. Then, I opined that instead praying that way, you should try in another way. Pray that you want to stay back in this same place to take care of your parents. Pray that your sister and her husband live together happily .

So basically, I opined that you should pray about what you desire. Not about what you do not want. You should be thankful to God with prayers about your preferences. Only then, will he show you the pathway to the resources you need to fulfil your wishes.

CHAPTER SIXTY-FIVE

Circumstances Change with Time

Every day gives you options to face the various challenges life throws at us. Instead of seeing those challenges as an obstacle, you should be ready to face them with your skill and talent. Do not lock yourself into the chain of depression. You should explore all possibilities for moving on.

When Jio was introduced into the Indian market, we thought that all other network companies would disappear. But, today, Airtel is the only company which withstood the storm and continues to give efficient service to their customers.

In any kind of situation or circumstance, you must believe in yourself to be able to stand up and face it. Because situations will change with time.

CHAPTER SIXTY-SIX

Fight the Situation

Most of the time, when you start a new thing or go to a new place, you tend to have a small fear in a corner of your heart. For eg. If you are driving a bike or a car. Suddenly you notice that one vehicle is following you. What do you do? You either increase your speed and try to drive away speedily. Otherwise you would decrease your speed and let the vehicle overtake you.

In the same way, when starting a new job or work, there will be a small hesitation in your mind about weather or not the job will set right appropriately or not.

In this way, you should notice and analyse every thought of yours. And take care not to let any negative thoughts rule your mind.

CHAPTER SIXTY-SEVEN

Two Small Formulas For Winning

Have you ever thought about someone in this way – how successful he is! Whatever work he is starting, it's turning into a grand success! In the same way, have you ever felt that whenever you start a work , it keeps dragging on and isn't being ready on time?

Everyone gets some opportunities. The difference is that you have been only noticing the challenges as problems. And they have been taking up the challenges as possibilities for success.

You have break the barriers of your imagination that you are surrounded by only difficulties and thorns. You have to keep on trying consistently. No one becomes successful overnight. The success formula as told by highly successful people is 1.Consistent effort. 2. Patience. Only these two qualities determine the key to success.

CHAPTER SIXTY-EIGHT

Things Could Be Difficult This Way

A person I know well, has a weird bad habit. He could lie without blinking an eye, to anyone, anywhere, be it office or neighbourhood. For eg. If he is asked," How come you have come all this way? Do you have some work around here? ". He would say,"yes, I have some work around here. I have come to meet someone here." Then in that case, if I offer to help him around to get somewhere, he would vehemently deny. But, after sometime, if you ask him about that day, he would describe a different story altogether.

According to him, he is doing things confidentially, but he fails to realise that he is dragging down his own reputation and the trust which people have in him.

This does not mean that you should share all your thoughts and circumstances with everyone around. Family matters are best discussed within family. Workplace issues are to be discussed with colleagues or the people you deem worthy of.

CHAPTER SIXTY-NINE

Learn New Things

Nowadays, lot of people are not ready to learn new things. No one is bothered about how much time we are all wasting each day. The time which we waste everyday can be utilised fruitfully if we try to learn new things.

Now, if a notification pops up in your smartphone for app updates, you readily update it. Then why are you not ready to update yourself? How much more time would you prefer to be out dated? You should learn a new thing to update yourself. For eg.

You can learn a new language or a musical instrument or a sport or any field in which you are interested in. If you do so, u will be enriching yourself with new talents and skills everyday. If you want to reach your ambition, then the journey of learning new things should never stop.

CHAPTER SEVENTY

Actions Speak Volumes

Do you remember the person or individual because of whom your life took a drastic turn? Or the person who was responsible for the moment which was the turning point of your life? That may be your teacher or a close friend or parents or any relative or a family friend or whoever it may be. That person is the one who had recognised your skills and had helped you to climb the ladder of your dreams.

Have you ever done anything for him/her in return? He/she might not have expected anything in return from you while guiding you back then. But, have you ever had the thought about how would you be useful to him? In the same way, have you ever extended similar kind or help to anyone? Have you been able to guide anyone without expectations?

CHAPTER SEVENTY-ONE

What is Your Reason?

Like all living beings, we humans too take birth and get to live on this planet. Instead of living an average life of waking up, eating and going back to sleep, you should think about how to add meaning to your life.

For that matter, it doesn't mean that only if you are a great leader or scientist can do something like that. Like everyone else, in the crowd, doing what everyone else is doing, living with no challenges in life, at lest look into what you can do for your next generation.

Whatever work or assets you carry on for your future generations, you would be satisfied and your family too will be proud of you. May be that is the reason of your existence.

CHAPTER SEVENTY-TWO

The One Thing That Will Definitely Follow You

Do you know what will follow you till the end? It's the fruit of your actions. The benefits of your good deeds or the fruit of your misdeeds. You have to decide the course of your actions, be it good or evil.

Even if you achieve great qualifications and settle in good jobs, in case of encountering a failure or loss, your mind becomes filled with insecurities and fear. If you keep accumulating the fear and without self confidence, negative thoughts keep seeding in your brain and this drives away your happiness. That's why, our ancestors have advised that even if someone does harm or evil to you, you should repay the person with some good deeds. Whatever situations happen to you, you should consciously choose to be optimistic. If you are continually optimistic, only good things will happen to you.

CHAPTER SEVENTY-THREE

Do Not Hesitate

If everyone has superpowers, there would be no problems at all. Everyone will definitely have a small hope in some corner of their hearts that they would be able to succeed in things. That is necessary. But, while implementing, they would doubt themselves, often overthinking about the circumstances and themselves. However, being overconfident is dangerous too. So, if you happen to get a small doubt, you must take advice from a person whom you would be able to help you or the person from whom you had taken inspiration. Do not fear that they would underestimate you. Asking for help and getting clarified regarding something is never wrong.

CHAPTER SEVENTY-FOUR

Dare To Achieve The Dream

One of my friend had an extraordinary dream to build 100 houses and earn rental income from it. One of our acquaintances replied,“ people do not have a single house to live in. How come you dream of a 100 houses. Don’t you think it’s an exorbitant dream of yours? ”. To this, my friend replied,“ I do not want my future generations to live in any kind of financial difficulties. I just want to leave them with some financial assistance after me.For that, I need to do this.". Then he asked again," Do you have enough finances to build 100 houses then"? My friend replied," some things may seem to be huge. But becoming intimidated by that is no way to go. We could break it into small achievable targets and plans. By implementing the small plans, we get to know the minute details of the job. All big businesses now, have once upon a time, started small. In the same concept, I built one house first. After 3 years, I built 3 more houses. Then after 5 years more, I built 6 houses. In this way, it took me 35 years to reach my target of building 100 houses. You have been only seeing the difficulties in the challenge. I have been searching for opportunities in the same challenge. "

Well, how about you? Would you dare to dream?

CHAPTER SEVENTY-FIVE

Do not be in this List

If someone asks you two qualities you like in your self, then you would answer it instantly. But if someone asks you two qualities which dislike in yourself, then you might think for 2secs and then answer. Isn't it? Then, what effort did you make to modify the qualities which you dislike?

One of my colleagues is my team member. He was quite a smart person. He would try and solve any kind of problem or assignment in the required time and submit it soon. Most people in my office knew well about him. His boss considered him his ‘right hand’. But, he would often arrive late to the office. Even for group meetings, he would show up at least 5 mins late. But, based on his performance at work, even the management doesn’t mind much about his bad punctuality.

Our HR had granted him an increment of 10%. But he was dissatisfied with it. According to him, he had done a great job through out the year and so he deserved a bigger increment. He even had a bit of argument with the HR regarding the same matter. To that the HR simply replied that,“ your increment recommendation has been issued and it is 10% only. You have lost your score in discipline and punctuality. ”

In my opinion, whatever be your talent or whoever you might be, being punctual is an impressive quality.

CHAPTER SEVENTY-SIX

Impossible Expectations

We all know that every person is equipped with a unique talent. But, when we communicate with others, we often to forget this fact.

One day, all the managers in my workplace came together and organised a meeting. The GM who presided the meeting, asked the relevant points according to his work status to each manager. He would ask each manager ," do you know what I would I have done if I was in your place? I would have done this the other way and the result would have been better." He would boast about himself.

When my turn came, he asked the same question. “As a senior employee in this company, what would you have done? ” I replied,“ Sir,I would send all the employees home, because you are the only one who can do all the work. A lot of cost can be saved to the company.

The next second his expression and tone changed. He ended the meeting saying that it wasn’t his intention to pressurise us or humiliate us.

Can you ever completely act like some else? Then how can you expect someone else to be exactly like you. Expectations of this kind are impossible.

CHAPTER SEVENTY-SEVEN

Try Asking This to Your Children

What are you giving more importance to in your life? If you have been thinking about work or business most of the time, the promotion and money resulting thus, will not give you may other things you need in life. If you are unmarried, ask your parents. Or if you have children, try asking them, " what is it that you do not like about me?" If you agree to what they answered, then are you willing to make efforts to change that in you? Or if that something is a misunderstanding, then try convincing them about it.

This kind of effort to bond will give you a beautiful relationship.

CHAPTER SEVENTY-EIGHT

There is A Way to Know Things

Usually, when you talk to someone, it may be about workplace or home, you ask questions in anticipation of some news you want to know. The other person might interrupt you and cross question you regarding something else. Then, if you too interrupt him and continue the same way, you might end up in a confusion of words and neither would be able to gather any information as expected.

Even if you have a lot to say, it is a good idea to pause and let the other person complete his sentence. If you speak out next, it will be a smooth exchange of information between you both. And may be, by being a good listener, you might be benefit from it.

CHAPTER SEVENTY-NINE

What a Magical Life

Don't you think it's pure greed to expect that everything you do will always be correct. But, there is nothing wrong in hoping that what you do should be right. However, it not humanely possible to be perfect every time. Sometimes, you will be confident enough that your attempt at something will go alright. But at the same time, having a small insecurity too is natural. You cannot do anything without an evaluation of self. It's your self esteem and confidence which will make a pathway for your success.

CHAPTER EIGHTY

Never Take Things For Granted

However you live, no matter what work you do, if you are disinterested in what you do, your life will become quite boring. People who haven't experienced defeat, should understand that failing will just serve as a step to your success. It's not that you are going to fail forever.

If u succumb to one failure, then your success story will belong to someone else. If recognition and fame is a sign of success, then you should consider even a failure as a sign of success.

CHAPTER EIGHTY-ONE

Creation and Destruction

We are naturally created to feel and experience various emotions. But most people neither give much attention to their own inner feelings nor to others feelings and emotions. Some people are naturally soft natured and generous. Such people are so sensitive that they even for things that generally generate anger and turmoil, they would react calm to it. If you see this, you would think," how come this person is handling such a big issue in such a calm way.But when it comes to minor situations, he is making it large by shouting and manhandling. You would have definitely met at least two people in your life who bear this kind of qualities. If I ask you which of the above two natured people would you like to deal with, you would obviously answer the person with the soft natured kind.

Because, his level headedness and soft nature are the qualities which make him approachable to people.

CHAPTER EIGHTY-TWO

All in One

Goodness and evil, pleasure and tragedy, happiness and sorrow, victory and failures, selfishness and selflessness... we face either of the above qualities in most people around. If any of these emotions influence us a little, we would be able manage them gracefully. Otherwise, why would start lamenting about why would God give us such a hard time. Our actions are the ones which determine which kind of emotions we would go through. We should self analyse our own actions and try to make amends. Otherwise, our life would be a ridiculous roller coaster of all kind of emotions which may be difficult for us to handle.

CHAPTER EIGHTY-THREE

Your Focus Should Be On Your Aim

Are you always dejected? Do you experience difficulties in whatever you do? Facing conflict in office, home and with customers? Does your work seem a never ending affair? At that point of time, you get a dejected feeling, questioning your fate, existence and destiny. In such kind of situation, you would feel that all your problems are getting together and pressurising you. But, you should be able to prioritise your problems and find solutions to each of them one after the other.

CHAPTER EIGHTY-FOUR

Your Day is based on

Generally people all over the world start their day with a newspaper and coffee. Well, how would your day go if you happen to start your day with a negative emotion or a bad sight. Nowadays, over 95% of the news published in newspapers is of the negative kind. You would read each news carefully all through and then your mind runs through all the negative emotions inflicted by the news.

Then, if you ask," should we not read the news?" Well, it's not so. If you happen to see a negative news, you might want to skip it for that moment. Gradually, you would get into a habit of searching for good news alone and reading it.

If possible, you should better stop reading news in the morning and keep it for leisure in the evening. Because if your day starts with good emotions, your day will be a happy one.

CHAPTER EIGHTY-FIVE

Change According To Age

Usually, in schools and colleges, we call our friends my some nicknames. And gradually, those names become a part of us. Even after we grow up, no matter how many pass away, if some old friends come across, they would still address us the same way.

Do not call yourself by a name which you do not like. If you feel regret when you are called by your nickname even after you grow up, u should let them know gently.

And in the same way, even you should take care that you must not hurt someone by addressing them by their nicknames.

CHAPTER EIGHTY-SIX

Encourage It If you Know That it is Better

Do you remember how you were around 10 years ago? Or even how you were 20 years ago.Our civilised life has showed a better way to live life today. This must be something which we should feel happy about.

Well, did you ever ask yourself if you still follow the good things that you once followed around 10years ago. We should not forget those things in the course of our life. In fact, we should nurture and encourage it.

It might be anything..being in a joint family, healthy food habits, physical fitness programs, whatever be it. The more you practice it, the more you promote it, the better it will be for you.

CHAPTER EIGHTY-SEVEN

You Must Know This

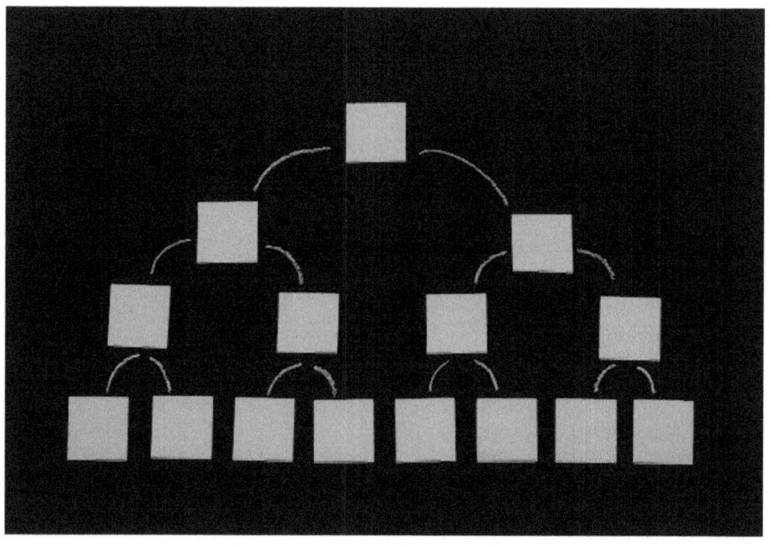

It's commonly seen in offices that some top executives want to have some hierarchy between them and their subordinates. They would like their subordinates to reach out to them and take permissions from them for almost anything. They are the persons who would fix the maximum reaching point for each of the subordinates. In case of product failures and customer escalations, they would even argue with their subordinates as to why it was not reported to them earlier. But in case the subordinates wanted to report earlier as a precautionary method, they would just direct them to their reporting boss. In short, they would be questioning their subordinates in any case, weather they do something or not. In such cases, acceptance is better than argument. Maintaining silence is advisable . Then, whenever the subordinates get a chance, they should clarify themselves to their seniors at once.

CHAPTER EIGHTY-EIGHT

Do What You Can

There are things you could have done more than earning well, eating well, sleeping well, earned well enough for our next generation. What have you done for the society you live in? This society is everything we are surrounded by. I had been to a friends' house recently. I noticed that in one corner of the house, he had kept some food and water for the birds. Only then, the thought came to me," in what way have I helped others?" It may be in any form. Giving a meal to the hungry or paying a month's fees to the needy child.. there are ,any kinds of needy people surrounding you. So, doing whatever you can will definitely count.

CHAPTER EIGHTY-NINE

Did you watch correctly?

Lot of people around us do not care much about their health. We can't say that we do not love our health. I'm not talking about going to gym or running or any dieting. Your financial and health condition will force you to think about getting yourself a health insurance policy. In this modern world, how much pre and healthy food are you able to take? Have you thought about that? Even Lot of people who exercise regularly, often end up in hospitals. If you have a health insurance, it will help you when extremely necessary. Youwon't even have to ask for help to others.

CHAPTER NINETY

Do Not Ever Waste

Have we ever used our full strength? Definitely never. Everyone one of us will have a way to display our strength to others. For eg. You are running in a race. You are putting your full effort and running along in the race. During running, are you having any other thought other than reaching the goal ? Obviously no. Your full focus will be on reaching the end point.

In that case, when you are doing some other work or performing some other job, how come your mind is becoming diverted on other things? Your focus alone will guide you through. So, when you are in some work, try to focus along. Do not divide your attention to other things.

CHAPTER NINETY-ONE

Do You Have This?

Do you feel happy only when your surroundings are in accordance to you?Or sometimes, even for situations which are not in accordance to you, are you able to deal with them with patience and tolerance?It's said that Thomas Alva Edison have faced failures for around a 1000 times before successfully inventing the light bulb. Even after multiple failures, he did not give up his curiosity and patience. That's what lead him to success.

What ever you face, success or failures, you should be prepared to face the next challenge with a smile on your face.

CHAPTER NINETY-TWO

I'm My Own Wealth

Sometimes, you might feel that you could not do anything, you are of no use to anyone, You have nothing to help others, no one likes you, no one likes what ever you do. But when you get such feelings, you should remember that you are your biggest wealth, you are your biggest treasure. A lot of people in this world have started from nothing and have erected huge empires. Haven't you noticed anyone like that? Hasn't anyone like that impressed you? You will be able to visualise only those things which you want. And that will be according to your thoughts. Because you are your own wealth.

CHAPTER NINETY-THREE

You Should Know This

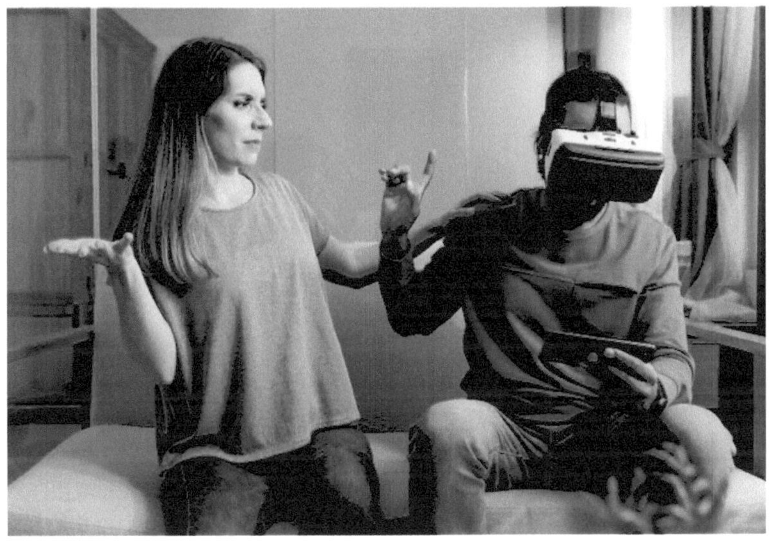

You should know how to talk and when to talk. Have you noticed it sometimes, that when you talk about something important to you without a gap, the other person would not pay any attention to you at all. At that point you need to understand two things. One is, if someone isn't paying attention to what you are speaking at all, then you should understand your value in that person's life. Second is, you should ask the opposite person if they have some time, so that you can talk. If the opposite person replies that he is free and that you may talk, but even then, if he didn't pay attention as you speak, then it will be wise on your part to get away from there saying,"thanks for your time."

CHAPTER NINETY-FOUR

All Are Not Your Friends

While you travel, you get to meet a person. Both of you introduce yourselves and start talking to talking to each other. He is talking freely to you and both of you are sharing your ideas and thoughts in a friendly manner.

Now, do you think it's wise on your part to share your personal or other things about yourself to a stranger? Not everyone whom you encounter can be your friend. At least, you should take sometime to meet people again and again, get to know them better, their habits and likes etc. at least for an year or so. Only then can you become friends.

But if you happen to freely share about yourself to every stranger, it might not be safe for you.

CHAPTER NINETY-FIVE

Beginning to End

Some people have the habit of completing the things compulsively once they started it. History states that such people have never seen failures. You might get a new idea and you search of ways to implement the idea and thus start a new business. While starting it, you should prepare a basic plan for it, determine the success rate, study the competition level and choose a business location. You must consider all the above points while planning to start a business. But, with just a plan in mind and no preparation, if you come half way through the journey and then plan of quitting it because you feel that it won't work out, then all you will face is the loss of time, money and energy. So, before you start anything, you need to build a concrete plan and then start.

CHAPTER NINETY-SIX

Keep Trying Till Victory

If you desperately need something, you need to keep trying for it. Opportunities will never come searching for you to knock your door. You need to decide what you want. For eg. If you want a good job, then choose the company you want to work for. You would then apply for it. After joining in the company, you will need to practice certain procedures to become an expert in the same. You would put your entire effort to get the job well done and qualify for a promotion.

So, you are putting your sincere efforts at your workplace. However, are you putting enough efforts to win up in life, just like at your workplace? Please try to think this way.

CHAPTER NINETY-SEVEN

You Too Are Human

Humans are just another life forms on this planet. Just like many other life forms. But, we humans have something called 6th sense which differentiates us from other living beings. We think that we have modernised the world a lot. But the ' panchabhootam' I.e earth, water, wind, sky and fire have never stopped teaching us that we are after all 'humans'.

CHAPTER NINETY-EIGHT

Make Decisions Intelligently

Please take decisions intelligently. When you are taking some decisions, please take care that you do not harm others. We all have different challenges at different phases of our life . At each phase, even if our decision does no good, take care that it does no harm to anyone either. Every individual's decision affects another individual in some or the other way.

CHAPTER NINETY-NINE

Be Brave

Do you have the bravery to take a huge challenge? If you have self doubt, it means that you have more fear than bravery. You are the person who has been feeding the fear with self doubt. Have you ever felt that way? Just give it a thought that you are learning how to ride a bicycle or swimming or driving a car, how was your heartbeat? It would be definitely be faster than normal. Why? The curiosity about the new thing, the confidence in yourself about learning it and the interest you show towards it all count for it. And your braveness increases double fold simultaneously.

About Author

This fascinating book authored by Lucas Lenin offers you a new vision of personal development which would enable you to assess Your Self Introspection. The society and the increasingly competitive world of work throw challenges at you every day. Combating them with unfaltering confidence is the sure-shot way to success. It is your personality that conveys to the world what you are. The 99A is a guide to the perfectly groomed and confident you.

It will help you become more realistic then before through a wide range of positive vibes and self realization.

Lucas Lenin is an Entrepreneur, a Life Coach and an experienced professional in training people to reach the state of Financial Freedom and he has experience more than 18 years in corporate various industries like Automotive, Printing & Packaging, Lubricants, Electronics & etc. He has various businesses like E-Learning, Retails, Agriculture, Logistics, Real Estate & Digital Marketing.

His passion is learning and Coaching, over the period of 18 Years corporate tenure, conducted 100+ training and helped thousands of people to develop their knowledge in core fields.

Lucas Lenin welcomes you to Learn More; Achieve More and Live Happiest Life style.

www.lucaslenin.com

www.ingramcontent.com/pod-product-compliance
Ingram Content Group UK Ltd.
Pitfield, Milton Keynes, MK11 3LW, UK
UKHW042018190726
13854UKWH00005B/2352